The Key Facts™ on

Armenia

Essential Information on Armenia

By Patrick W. Nee

The Internationalist®

www.internationalist.com

The Internationalist®

International Business, Investment, and Travel

Published by:

The Internationalist Publishing Company

96 Walter Street/ Suite 200

Boston, MA 02131, USA

Tel: 617-354-7722

www.internationalist.com

PN@internationalist.com

Table Of Contents

Chapter 1: Background

Armenia prides itself on being the first nation to formally adopt Christianity (early 4th century). Despite periods of autonomy, over the centuries Armenia came under the sway of various empires including the Roman, Byzantine, Arab, Persian, and Ottoman. During World War I in the western portion of Armenia, Ottoman Turkey instituted a policy of forced resettlement coupled with other harsh practices that resulted in at least 1 million Armenian deaths. The eastern area of Armenia was ceded by the Ottomans to Russia in 1828; this portion declared its independence in 1918, but was conquered by the Soviet Red Army in 1920. Armenian leaders remain preoccupied by the long conflict with Azerbaijan over Nagorno-Karabakh, a primarily Armenian-populated region, assigned to Soviet Azerbaijan in the 1920s by Moscow. Armenia and Azerbaijan began fighting over the area in 1988; the struggle escalated after both countries attained independence from the Soviet Union in 1991. By May 1994, when a cease-fire took hold, ethnic Armenian forces held not only Nagorno-Karabakh but also a significant portion of Azerbaijan proper. The economies of both sides have been hurt by their inability to make substantial progress toward a peaceful resolution. Turkey closed the common border with Armenia in 1993 in support of

Azerbaijan in its conflict with Armenia over control of Nagorno-Karabakh and surrounding areas, further hampering Armenian economic growth. In 2009, senior Armenian leaders began pursuing rapprochement with Turkey, aiming to secure an opening of the border, but Turkey has not yet ratified the Protocols normalizing relations between the two countries. In September 2013, President SARGSIAN announced Armenia will join Russia, Belarus, and Kazakhstan as a member of the Customs Union.

Chapter 2: Geography

Location:

Southwestern Asia, between Turkey (to the west) and Azerbaijan

Geographic coordinates:

40 00 N, 45 00 E

Map references:

Middle East

Area:

total: 29,743 sq km

country comparison to the world: 143

land: 28,203 sq km

water: 1,540 sq km

Area - comparative:

slightly smaller than Maryland

Land boundaries:

total: 1,254 km

border countries: Azerbaijan-proper 566 km, Azerbaijan-Naxcivan exclave 221 km, Georgia 164 km, Iran 35 km, Turkey 268 km

Coastline:

0 km (landlocked)

Maritime claims:

none (landlocked)

Climate:

> highland continental, hot summers, cold winters

Terrain:

> Armenian Highland with mountains; little forest land; fast flowing rivers; good soil in Aras River valley

Elevation extremes:

> lowest point: Debed River 400 m

> highest point: Aragats Lerrnagagat' 4,090 m

Natural resources:

> small deposits of gold, copper, molybdenum, zinc, bauxite

Land use:

> arable land: 14.47%

> permanent crops: 1.8%

> other: 83.74% (2011)

Irrigated land:

> 2,735 sq km (2006)

Total renewable water resources:

> 7.77 cu km (2011)

Freshwater withdrawal (domestic/industrial/agricultural):

> total: 2.86 cu km/yr (40%/6%/54%)

> per capita: 929.7 cu m/yr (2010)

Natural hazards:

> occasionally severe earthquakes; droughts

Environment - current issues:

soil pollution from toxic chemicals such as DDT; the energy crisis of the 1990s led to deforestation when citizens scavenged for firewood; pollution of Hrazdan (Razdan) and Aras Rivers; the draining of Sevana Lich (Lake Sevan), a result of its use as a source for hydropower, threatens drinking water supplies; restart of Metsamor nuclear power plant in spite of its location in a seismically active zone

Environment - international agreements:

party to: Air Pollution, Biodiversity, Climate Change, Climate Change-Kyoto Protocol, Desertification, Environmental Modification, Hazardous Wastes, Law of the Sea, Ozone Layer Protection, Wetlands
signed, but not ratifiedAir Pollution-Persistent Organic Pollutants

Geography - note:

landlocked in the Lesser Caucasus Mountains; Sevana Lich (Lake Sevan) is the largest lake in this mountain range

Chapter 3: People and Society

Nationality:

noun: Armenian(s)

adjective: Armenian

Ethnic groups:

Armenian 98.1%, Yezidi (Kurd) 1.1%, other 0.7% (2011 est.)

Languages:

Armenian (official) 97.9%, Kurdish (spoken by Yezidi minority) 1%, other 1% (2011 est.)

Religions:

Armenian Apostolic 92.6%, Evangelical 1%, other 2.4%, none 1.1%, unspecified 2.9% (2011 est.)

Population:

3,060,631 (July 2014 est.)

country comparison to the world: 137

Age structure:

0-14 years: 19.1% (male 312,955/female 272,065)

15-24 years: 15.2% (male 236,317/female 228,943)

25-54 years: 43.5% (male 638,141/female 693,397)

55-64 years: 10.5% (male 161,102/female 195,714)

65 years and over: 9.8% (male 128,568/female 193,429)

(2014 est.)

Dependency ratios:

> total dependency ratio: 44.1%
>
> youth dependency ratio: 29.2%
>
> elderly dependency ratio: 14.9%
>
> potential support ratio: 6.7% (2013)

Median age:

> total: 33.7 years
>
> male: 31.8 years
>
> female: 35.8 years (2014 est.)

Population growth rate:

> -0.13% (2014 est.)
>
> country comparison to the world: 209

Birth rate:

> 13.92 births/1,000 population (2014 est.)
>
> country comparison to the world: 143

Death rate:

> 9.3 deaths/1,000 population (2014 est.)
>
> country comparison to the world: 62

Net migration rate:

> -5.88 migrant(s)/1,000 population (2014 est.)
>
> country comparison to the world: 197

Urbanization:

> urban population: 64.1% of total population (2011)
>
> rate of urbanization: 0.34% annual rate of change (2010-15 est.)

Major urban areas - population:

YEREVAN (capital) 1.116 million (2011)

Sex ratio:

at birth: 1.14 male(s)/female

0-14 years: 1.15 male(s)/female

15-24 years: 1.03 male(s)/female

25-54 years: 0.92 male(s)/female

55-64 years: 0.93 male(s)/female

65 years and over: 0.59 male(s)/female

total population: 0.89 male(s)/female (2014 est.)

Mother's mean age at first birth:

24.1

note: median age at first birth among women 25-29 (2010 est.)

Maternal mortality rate:

30 deaths/100,000 live births (2010)

country comparison to the world: 124

Infant mortality rate:

total: 13.97 deaths/1,000 live births

country comparison to the world: 113

male: 15.39 deaths/1,000 live births

female: 12.36 deaths/1,000 live births (2014 est.)

Life expectancy at birth:

> total population: 74.12 years
>
> country comparison to the world: 116
>
> male: 70.9 years
>
> female: 77.78 years (2014 est.)

Total fertility rate:

> 1.64 children born/woman (2014 est.)
>
> country comparison to the world: 117

Contraceptive prevalence rate:

> 54.9% (2010)

Health expenditures:

> 4.3% of GDP (2011)
>
> country comparison to the world: 156

Physicians density:

> 2.85 physicians/1,000 population (2011)

Hospital bed density:

> 4 beds/1,000 population (2011)

Drinking water source:

> improved:
>
>> *urban*: 99.6% of population
>>
>> *rural*: 98.4% of population
>>
>> *total*: 99.2% of population
>
> unimproved:
>
>> *urban*: 0.4% of population
>>
>> *rural*: 1.6% of population
>>
>> *total*: 0.8% of population (2011 est.)

Sanitation facility access:

improved:

urban: 95.9% of population

rural: 80.5% of population

total: 90.4% of population

unimproved:

urban: 4.1% of population

rural: 19.5% of population

total: 9.6% of population (2011 est.)

HIV/AIDS - adult prevalence rate:

0.2% (2012)

country comparison to the world: 105

HIV/AIDS - people living with HIV/AIDS:

3,500 (2012)

country comparison to the world: 130

HIV/AIDS - deaths:

200 (2012)

country comparison to the world: 106

Obesity - adult prevalence rate:

24% (2008)

country comparison to the world: 68

Children under the age of 5 underweight:

5.3% (2010)

country comparison to the world: 89

Education expenditures:

3.3% of GDP (2012)

country comparison to the world: 132

Literacy:

definition: age 15 and over can read and write

total population: 99.6%

male: 99.7%

female: 99.5% (2011 est.)

School life expectancy (primary to tertiary education):

total: 12 years

male: 11 years

female: 14 years (2009)

Child labor – children ages 5-14:

total number: 19,596

percentage: 4%

note: data represents children ages 7-17 (2007 est.)

Unemployment, youth ages 15-24:

total: 29.1%

country comparison to the world: 29

male: 29.6%

female: 28.6% (2011)

Chapter 4: Government and Key Leaders

Country name:

conventional long form: Republic of Armenia

conventional short form: Armenia

local long form: Hayastani Hanrapetut'yun

local short form: Hayastan

former: Armenian Soviet Socialist Republic, Armenian Republic

Government type:

republic

Capital:

name: Yerevan

geographic coordinates: 40 10 N, 44 30 E

time difference: UTC+4 (9 hours ahead of Washington, DC during Standard Time)

Administrative divisions:

11 provinces (marzer, singular - marz); Aragatsotn, Ararat, Armavir, Geghark'unik', Kotayk', Lorri, Shirak, Syunik', Tavush, Vayots' Dzor, Yerevan

Independence:

21 September 1991 (from the Soviet Union)

National holiday:

Independence Day, 21 September (1991)

Constitution:

previous 1915, 1978; latest adopted 5 July 1995; amended 2005 (2013)

Legal system:

civil law system

International law organization participation:

has not submitted an ICJ jurisdiction declaration; non-party state to the ICCt

Suffrage:

18 years of age; universal

Executive branch:

chief of state: President Serzh SARGSIAN (since 9 April 2008)

head of government: Prime Minister Tigran SARGSIAN (since 9 April 2008)

cabinet: Council of Ministers appointed by the prime minister

elections: president elected by popular vote for a five-year term (eligible for a second term); election last held on 18 February 2013 (next to be held February 2018); prime minister appointed by the president based on majority or plurality support in parliament; the prime minister and Council of Ministers must resign if the National Assembly refuses to accept their program

election results: Serzh SARGSIAN reelected president;
percent of vote - Serzh SARGSIAN 58.6%, Raffi
HOVHANNISIAN 36.7%, Hrant BAGRATIAN 2.2%,
other 2.5%

Legislative branch:

unicameral National Assembly (Parliament) or Azgayin
Zhoghov (131 seats; members elected by popular vote, 90
members elected by party list and 41 by direct vote; to
serve five-year terms)

elections: last held on 6 May 2012 (next to be held in the
spring of 2017)

election results: percent of vote by party - RPA 44%,
Prosperous Armenia 30.1%, ANC 7.1%, Heritage Party
5.8%, ARF (Dashnak) 5.7%, Rule of Law 5.5%, other
1.8%; seats by party - RPA 69, Prosperous Armenia 37,
ANC 7, Heritage Party 5, ARF (Dashnak) 5, Rule of Law
6, independent 2

Judicial branch:

Highest court(s): Court of Cassation (consists of the court
chairman and organized into a criminal chamber and a
civil and administrative chamber, each with a court
chairman and 2 judges); Constitutional Court (consists of 9
judges)

Judge selection and term of offfice: Court of Cassation judges nominated by the Judicial Council, a 9-member body of selected judges and legal scholars; judges appointed by the president; Constitutional Court judges - 4 appointed by the president, and 5 elected by National Assembly; judges of both courts can serve until retirement at age 65

subordinate courts: 2 Courts of Appeal (for civil cases and for criminal and military cases); district courts; Administrative Court

Political parties and leaders:

Armenian National Congress or ANC (bloc of independent and opposition parties) [Levon TER-PETROSSIAN]

Armenian National Movement or ANM [Ararat ZURABIAN]

Armenian Revolutionary Federation ("Dashnak" Party) or ARF [Hrant MARKARIAN]

Heritage Party [Raffi HOVHANNISIAN]

People's Party of Armenia [Stepan DEMIRCHIAN]

Prosperous Armenia [Gagik TSARUKIAN]

Republican Party of Armenia or RPA [Serzh SARGSIAN]

Rule of Law Party (Orinats Yerkir) [Artur BAGHDASARIAN]

Political pressure groups and leaders:

Aylentrank (Impeachment Alliance) [Nikol PASHINIAN]

Yerkrapah Union [Manvel GRIGORIAN]

International organization participation:

ADB, BSEC, CD, CE, CIS, CSTO, EAEC (observer), EAPC, EBRD, FAO, GCTU, IAEA, IBRD, ICAO, ICC (NGOs), ICRM, IDA, IFAD, IFC, IFRCS, ILO, IMF, Interpol, IOC, IOM, IPU, ISO, ITSO, ITU, MIGA, NAM (observer), OAS (observer), OIF, OPCW, OSCE, PFP, UN, UNCTAD, UNESCO, UNIDO, UNIFIL, UNWTO, UPU, WCO, WFTU (NGOs), WHO, WIPO, WMO, WTO

Diplomatic representation in the US:

chief of mission: Ambassador Tatoul MARKARIAN (since 26 May 2005)

chancery: 2225 R Street NW, Washington, DC 20008

telephone: [1] (202) 319-1976

FAX: [1] (202) 319-2982

consulate(s) general: Glendale (CA), Los Angeles

Diplomatic representation from the US:

chief of mission: Ambassador John HEFFERN (since 6 October 2011)

embassy: 1 American Ave., Yerevan 0082

mailing address: American Embassy Yerevan, US Department of State, 7020 Yerevan Place, Washington, DC 20521-7020

telephone: [374](10) 464-700

FAX: [374](10) 464-742

Key Leaders:

Pres.	Serzh SARGSIAN
Prime Min.	Tigran SARGSIAN
President's Chief of Staff	Vigen SARGSIAN
Min. of Agriculture	Sergo KARAPETIAN
Min. of Culture & Youth	Hasmik POGHOSIAN
Min. of Defense	Seyran OHANIAN
Min. of Diaspora	Hranush HAKOBIAN
Min. of Economy	Vahram AVANESIAN
Min. of Education & Science	Armen ASHOTIAN
Min. of Emergency Situations	Armen YERITSIAN
Min. of Energy & Natural Resources	Armen MOVSISIAN
Min. of Environmental Protection	Aram HARUTYUNIAN
Min. of Finance	David SARGSIAN
Min. of Foreign Affairs	Eduard NALBANDIAN
Min. of Health	Derenik DUMANIAN
Min. of Justice	Hrayr TOVMASIAN
Min. of Labor & Social Affairs	Artem ASATRIAN
Min. of Sport & Youth Affairs	Yuri VARDANIAN
Min. of Territorial Admin.	Armen GEVORGIAN
Min. of Transport & Communication	Gagik BEGLARIAN
Min. of Urban Development	Samvel TADEVOSIAN
Chmn., Central Bank of Armenia	Artur JAVADIAN
Ambassador to the US	Tatoul MARKARIAN
Permanent Representative to the UN, New York	Garen NAZARIAN

Flag description:

three equal horizontal bands of red (top), blue, and orange; the color red recalls the blood shed for liberty, blue the

Armenian skies as well as hope, and orange the land and
the courage of the workers who farm it

National symbol(s):

Mount Ararat; eagle; lion

National anthem:

name: "Mer Hayrenik""(Our Fatherland)

lyrics/music: Mikael NALBANDIAN/Barsegh
KANACHYAN

note: adopted 1991; based on the anthem of the
Democratic Republic of Armenia (1918-1922) but with
different lyrics

Chapter 5: Economy

Economy - overview:

After several years of double-digit economic growth, Armenia faced a severe economic recession with GDP declining more than 14% in 2009, despite large loans from multilateral institutions. Sharp declines in the construction sector and workers' remittances, particularly from Russia, led the downturn. The economy began to recover in 2010 with 2.1% growth, and has grown even faster in the three years since then. Under the old Soviet central planning system, Armenia developed a modern industrial sector, supplying machine tools, textiles, and other manufactured goods to sister republics, in exchange for raw materials and energy. Armenia has since switched to small-scale agriculture and away from the large agroindustrial complexes of the Soviet era. Armenia's geographic isolation, a narrow export base, and pervasive monopolies in important business sectors have made it particularly vulnerable to the sharp deterioration in the global economy and the economic downturn in Russia. Since August 2011, Armenia has experienced a sharp currency depreciation. Armenia has only two open trade borders - Iran and Georgia - because its borders with Azerbaijan and Turkey have been closed since 1991 and 1993, respectively, as a result of Armenia's ongoing conflict with Azerbaijan over the separatist Nagorno-Karabakh region. Armenia is particularly dependent on Russian commercial and governmental support and most key Armenian infrastructure is Russian-owned and/or managed, especially in the energy sector. The electricity distribution system was privatized in 2002 and bought by Russia's RAO-UES in 2005. Natural gas is primarily imported from Russia but construction of a pipeline to deliver natural gas from Iran to Armenia was completed in December 2008, and gas deliveries expanded after the April 2010 completion of the Yerevan Thermal Power Plant. Armenia's severe trade imbalance has been offset somewhat by international aid, remittances from Armenians working abroad, and foreign direct investment. Armenia joined the WTO in January 2003. The government made some improvements in tax and customs administration in recent years, but anti-corruption measures have been ineffective and the economic downturn has led to a sharp drop in tax revenue and forced the government to accept large loan packages from Russia, the IMF, and other international financial institutions. Amendments to tax legislation, including the introduction of the first ever "luxury tax" in 2011, aim to increase the ratio of budget revenues to GDP, which still remains at low levels. Armenia will need to pursue additional economic reforms and to strengthen the rule of law in order to regain economic growth and improve economic competitiveness and employment opportunities, especially given its economic isolation from two of its nearest neighbors, Turkey and Azerbaijan.

GDP (purchasing power parity):

$20.61 billion (2013 est.)

country comparison to the world: 133

$19.7 billion (2012 est.)

$18.38 billion (2011 est.)

note: data are in 2013 US dollars

GDP (official exchange rate):

$10.44 billion (2013 est.)

GDP - real growth rate:

4.6% (2013 est.)

country comparison to the world: 65

7.2% (2012 est.)

4.7% (2011 est.)

GDP - per capita (PPP):

$6,300 (2013 est.)

country comparison to the world: 147

$6,000 (2012 est.)

$5,600 (2011 est.)

note: data are in 2013 US dollars

Gross national saving:

16.2% of GDP (2013 est.)

country comparison to the world: 104

13.2% of GDP (2012 est.)

16.1% of GDP (2011 est.)

GDP – composition, by end use:

household consumption: 84.7%

government consumption: 13%

investment in fixed capital: 22.7%

investment in inventories: -0.9%

exports of goods and services: 23.6%

imports of goods and services: -43.1% (2013 est.)

GDP - composition by sector:

agriculture: 20.6%

industry: 37.3%

services: 42.1% (2013 est.)

Agriculture – products:

fruit (especially grapes), vegetables; livestock

Industries:

diamond-processing, metal-cutting machine tools, forging-pressing machines, electric motors, tires, knitted wear, hosiery, shoes, silk fabric, chemicals, trucks, instruments, microelectronics, jewelry manufacturing, software development, food processing, brandy, mining

Industrial production growth rate:

3.9% (2013 est.)

country comparison to the world: 77

Labor force:

1.394 million (2013 est.)

country comparison to the world: 133

Labor force - by occupation:

agriculture: 44.2%

industry: 16.8%

services: 39% (2008 est.)

Unemployment rate:

17.3% (2012 est.)

country comparison to the world: 153

18.4% (2011 est.)

Population below poverty line:

35.8% (2010 est.)

Household income or consumption by percentage share:

lowest 10%: 3.7%

highest 10%: 25.4% (2008)

Distribution of family income - Gini index:

30.9 (2008)

country comparison to the world: 115

44.4 (1996)

Budget:

revenues: $2.677 billion

expenditures: $2.707 billion (2013 est.)

Taxes and other revenues:

25.6% of GDP (2013 est.)

country comparison to the world: 119

Budget surplus (+) or deficit (-):

-0.3% of GDP (2013 est.)

country comparison to the world: 50

Public debt:

37.7% of GDP (2013 est.)

country comparison to the world: 98

41.4% of GDP (2012 est.)

Inflation rate (consumer prices):

6.2% (2013 est.)

country comparison to the world: 178

2.6% (2012 est.)

Central bank discount rate:

8% (11 January 2012)

country comparison to the world: 37

7.25% (2 December 2008)

note: this is the Refinancing Rate, the key monetary policy instrument of the Armenian National Bank

Commercial bank prime lending rate:

16.5% (31 December 2013 est.)

country comparison to the world: 28

17.23% (31 December 2012 est.)

note: average lending rate on loans up to one year

Stock of narrow money:

$1.418 billion (31 December 2013 est.)

country comparison to the world: 141

$1.352 billion (31 December 2012 est.)

Stock of broad money:

$2.051 billion (31 December 2013 est.)

country comparison to the world: 148

$1.829 billion (31 December 2012 est.)

Stock of domestic credit:

$4.355 billion (31 December 2012 est.)

country comparison to the world: 119

$3.548 billion (31 December 2011 est.)

Market value of publicly traded shares:

$132.1 million (31 December 2012 est.)

country comparison to the world: 118

$139.6 million (31 December 2011)

$144.8 million (31 December 2010 est.)

Current account balance:

-$720.6 million (2013 est.)

country comparison to the world: 112

-$1.052 billion (2012 est.)

Exports:

$1.653 billion (2013 est.)

country comparison to the world: 144

$1.588 billion (2012 est.)

Exports - commodities:

pig iron, unwrought copper, nonferrous metals, diamonds, mineral products, foodstuffs, energy

Exports - partners:

Russia 19.6%, Germany 10.7%, Bulgaria 9.1%, Belgium 8.9%, Iran 6.9%, US 6.1%, Canada 6%, Georgia 5.7%, Netherlands 5.6%, Switzerland 5% (2012)

Imports:

$3.459 billion (2013 est.)

country comparison to the world: 140

$3.656 billion (2012 est.)

Imports - commodities:

natural gas, petroleum, tobacco products, foodstuffs, diamonds

Imports - partners:

Russia 20%, Germany 11%, Bulgaria 9%, Belgium 9%, Iran 6.5%, US 6.1%, Canada 5.9%, Netherlands 5.6%, Georgia 5.6%, Switzerland 5.2% (2012 est.)

Reserves of foreign exchange and gold:

$1.863 billion (31 December 2013 est.)

country comparison to the world: 125

$1.799 billion (31 December 2012 est.)

Debt - external:

$7.839 billion (31 December 2013 est.)

country comparison to the world: 106

$7.633 billion (31 December 2012 est.)

Exchange rates:

Drams (AMD) per US dollar -

410.5 (2013 est.)

401.76 (2012 est.)

373.66 (2010 est.)

363.28 (2009)

303.93 (2008)

Chapter 6: Energy

Electricity - production:

      7.432 billion kWh (2011 est.)

      country comparison to the world: 103

Electricity - consumption:

      5.8 billion kWh (2011 est.)

      country comparison to the world: 108

Electricity - exports:

      1.36 billion kWh (2011 est.)

      country comparison to the world: 52

Electricity - imports:

      246 million kWh (2010 est.)

      country comparison to the world: 85

Electricity - installed generating capacity:

      3.472 million kW (2010 est.)

      country comparison to the world: 84

Electricity - from fossil fuels:

      55.6% of total installed capacity (2010 est.)

      country comparison to the world: 142

Electricity - from nuclear fuels:

      10.8% of total installed capacity (2010 est.)

      country comparison to the world: 16

Electricity - from hydroelectric plants:

      33.5% of total installed capacity (2010 est.)

      country comparison to the world: 67

Electricity - from other renewable sources:

0.1% of total installed capacity (2010 est.)

country comparison to the world: 106

Crude oil - production:

0 bbl/day (2013 est.)

country comparison to the world: 149

Crude oil - exports:

0 bbl/day (2013 est.)

country comparison to the world: 77

Crude oil - imports:

0 bbl/day (2013 est.)

country comparison to the world: 152

Crude oil - proved reserves:

0 bbl (1 January 2013 es)

country comparison to the world: 103

Refined petroleum products - production:

0 bbl/day (2013 est.)

country comparison to the world: 118

Refined petroleum products - consumption:

45,300 bbl/day (2011 est.)

country comparison to the world: 102

Refined petroleum products - exports:

31.78 bbl/day (2010 est.)

country comparison to the world: 124

Refined petroleum products - imports:

46,550 bbl/day (2010 est.)

country comparison to the world:72

Natural gas - production:

0 cu m (2013 est.)

country comparison to the world: 98

Natural gas - consumption:

2.1 billion cu m (2013 est.)

country comparison to the world: 78

Natural gas - exports:

0 cu m (2013 est.)

country comparison to the world: 57

Natural gas - imports:

2.1 billion cu m (2013 est.)

country comparison to the world: 47

Natural gas - proved reserves:

0 cu m (1 January 2013 es)

country comparison to the world: 109

Carbon dioxide emissions from consumption of energy:

11.74 million Mt (2011 est.)

country comparison to the world: 98

Chapter 7: Communications

Telephones - main lines in use:

584,000 (2012)

country comparison to the world: 92

Telephones - mobile cellular:

3.223 million (2012)

country comparison to the world: 128

Telephone system:

general assessment: telecommunications investments have made major inroads in modernizing and upgrading the outdated telecommunications network inherited from the Soviet era; now 100% privately owned and undergoing modernization and expansion; mobile-cellular services monopoly terminated in late 2004 and a second provider began operations in mid-2005

domestic: reliable modern fixed-line and mobile-cellular services are available across Yerevan in major cities and towns; significant but ever-shrinking gaps remain in mobile-cellular coverage in rural areas

<u>international</u>: country code - 374; Yerevan is connected to the Trans-Asia-Europe fiber-optic cable through Iran; additional international service is available by microwave radio relay and landline connections to the other countries of the Commonwealth of Independent States, through the Moscow international switch, and by satellite to the rest of the world; satellite earth stations - 3 (2008)

Broadcast media:

2 public TV networks operating alongside more than 40 privately owned TV stations that provide local to near nationwide coverage; major Russian broadcast stations are widely available; subscription cable TV services are available in most regions; Public Radio of Armenia is a national, state-run broadcast network that operates alongside about 20 privately owned radio stations; several major international broadcasters are available (2008)

Internet country code:

.am

Internet hosts:

194,142 (2012)

<u>country comparison to the world</u>: 73

Internet users:

208,200 (2009)

<u>country comparison to the world</u>: 138

Chapter 8: Transportation

Airports:

> 11 (2013)

> country comparison to the world: 154

Airports - with paved runways:

> total: 10

> over 3,047 m: 2

> 2,438 to 3,047 m: 2

> 1,524 to 2,437 m: 4

> 914 to 1,523 m: 2 (2013)

Airports - with unpaved runways:

> total: 1

> 914 to 1,523 m: 1 (2013)

Pipelines:

> gas 2,233 km (2013)

Railways:

> total: 869 km

> country comparison to the world: 96

> broad gauge: 869 km 1.520-m gauge (818 km electrified)

> note: some lines are out of service (2009)

Roadways:

> total: 7,705 km (2012)

> country comparison to the world: 143

Chapter 9: Military

Military branches:

Armenian Armed Forces: Ground Forces, Air Force and Air Defense; "Nagorno-Karabakh Republic": Nagorno-Karabakh Self-Defense Force (NKSDF) (2011)

Military service age and obligation:

18-27 years of age for voluntary or compulsory military service; 2-year conscript service obligation; 17 year olds are eligible to become cadets at military higher education institutes, where they are classified as military personnel (2012)

Manpower available for military service:

males age 16-49: 805,847

females age 16-49: 854,296 (2010 est.)

Manpower fit for military service:

males age 16-49: 644,372

females age 16-49: 717,272 (2010 est.)

Manpower reaching militarily significant age annually:

male: 23,470

female: 21,417 (2010 est.)

Military expenditures:

3.92% of GDP (2012)

country comparison to the world: 12

3.07 of GDP (2011)

3.92% of GDP (2010)

Chapter 10: Transnational Issues

Disputes - international:

the dispute over the break-away Nagorno-Karabakh region and the Armenian military occupation of surrounding lands in Azerbaijan remains the primary focus of regional instability; residents have evacuated the former Soviet-era small ethnic enclaves in Armenia and Azerbaijan; Turkish authorities have complained that blasting from quarries in Armenia might be damaging the medieval ruins of Ani, on the other side of the Arpacay valley; in 2009, Swiss mediators facilitated an accord reestablishing diplomatic ties between Armenia and Turkey, but neither side has ratified the agreement and the rapprochement effort has faltered; local border forces struggle to control the illegal transit of goods and people across the porous, undemarcated Armenian, Azerbaijani, and Georgian borders; ethnic Armenian groups in the Javakheti region of Georgia seek greater autonomy from the Georgian Government

Refugees and internally displaced persons:

refugees (country of origin): 6,000 (Syria - ethnic Armenians) (2013)

IDPs: 8,400 (conflict with Azerbaijan over Nagorno-Karabakh) (2009)

stateless persons: 35 (2012)

Illicit drugs:

illicit cultivation of small amount of cannabis for domestic consumption; minor transit point for illicit drugs - mostly opium and hashish - moving from Southwest Asia to Russia and to a lesser extent the rest of Europe

Map of Armenia

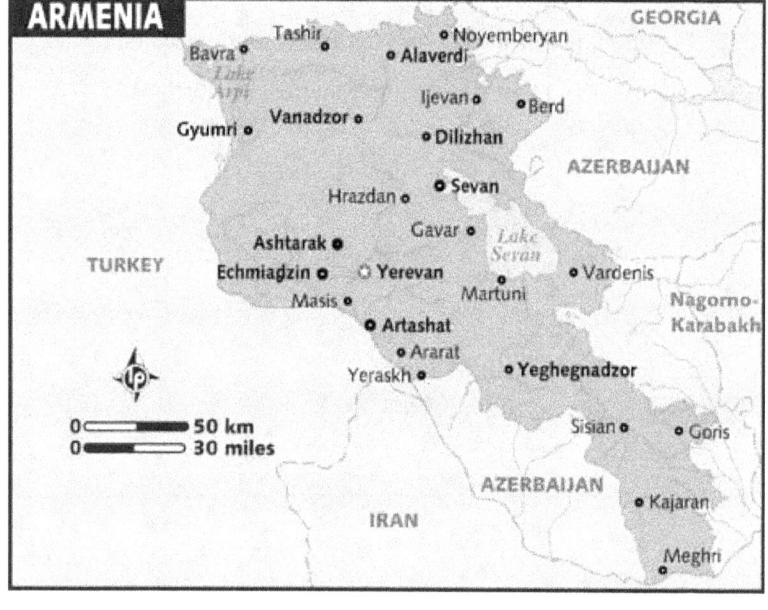

Other Key Facts™ Titles

Key Facts on South Korea

Key Facts on France

Key Facts on the United Kingdom

Key Facts on Egypt

Key Facts on Israel

All Key Facts™ Titles are Available at

www.Amazon.com

THE INTERNATIONALIST®

2014

WWW.INTERNATIONALIST.COM

www.ingramcontent.com/pod-product-compliance
Lightning Source LLC
Chambersburg PA
CBHW071808200526
45167CB00017B/1527